ON THE HUNT WITH
GRAY WOLVES

BY NANCY FURSTINGER

Published by The Child's World®
1980 Lookout Drive • Mankato, MN 56003-1705
800-599-READ • www.childsworld.com

Acknowledgments
The Child's World®: Mary Berendes, Publishing Director
Red Line Editorial: Design, editorial direction, and production
Photographs ©: Keith Szafranski/iStockphoto, cover, 1, 8; Tom Tietz/
iStockphoto/Thinkstock, 4; Alan Jeffery/Shutterstock Images, 6; JZ
Hunt/iStockphoto, 7; A. von Dueren/Shutterstock Images, 10; Debbie
Steinhausser/Shutterstock Images, 11; Jim Kruger/iStockphoto, 12; Red Line
Editorial, 14; Ronnie Howard/Shutterstock Images, 15; Shutterstock Images,
16, 21; Dan Cardiff/iStockphoto, 17; Holly Kuchera/Shutterstock Images, 18;
Dennis W. Donohue/Shutterstock Images, 20

ISBN 9781634074506

LCCN 2015946215

Printed in the United States of America
Mankato, MN
December, 2015
PA02279

TABLE OF CONTENTS

Chapter 1

NIGHTTIME HUNT

A big gray wolf wakes up just as the night begins. He slowly stretches and yawns. Then he points his nose up and howls. The howl signals his pack, or group. Soon the other gray wolves wake up. They all start howling. Each wolf has a special howl. These howls send out a signal to others in the pack. It is time to hunt.

One large male leads the way. He holds his tail high. This lets the other wolves know his rank, or place of importance in the group. He is the **alpha** male. His **mate** is the alpha female. She trots beside him. Gray wolves travel together in packs. All wolf packs have a leader. The alpha male is the leader. He is the strongest wolf. He is also the smartest.

Six other adult wolves follow the alpha pair into the mountains. They hunt in a group. They also work together to raise pups, or young wolves. One female adult stays at the **den**. She has a key

◄ **The alpha male's howl lets the members of his pack know it's time to hunt.**

▲ **Most gray wolf packs have between four and nine wolves.**

job. This wolf watches over the five pups. The alpha female gave birth to the pups that spring. Female and male adults take turns watching the pups.

The eight wolves in the hunting pack pick up speed. They travel down the mountain. A full moon rises. It lights up the valley below. The pack sprints for 30 miles (48 km). Wolves can run at speeds up to 40 miles (64 km) per hour.

Then the alpha male pauses. He sniffs the air. It is scented with pine and something else. He pricks up his ears. His keen senses make him the best hunter in the pack. Now the alpha male spots his **prey**. A lone moose calf stands in a lake. The young calf nibbles water plants. His mother is nowhere in sight. Wolves prey on big animals. They eat large **mammals** with hooves. Their main prey is bison, deer, elk, and moose. Wolves seek out prey that is young, sick, or old. These types of prey are easier to catch.

The wolf pack waits. Their leader creeps down to the lake. He jumps into the water. Then the rest of the pack follows. The wolves are strong swimmers. They circle the calf. The moose bellows with fear. He charges out of the water. But the wolves surround him. One leaps up and grabs the calf's nose. His mouth digs into the flesh. Then the pack tackles the calf. They use their strong jaws to bring him down. It has been a successful hunt.

▲ **Moose calves make good prey because they are not as skilled at escaping hunting gray wolves.**

Chapter 2

GRAY WOLF PUPS

The alpha wolf pair eats first. This is how all wolf packs work. A younger male tries to grab some meat. One alpha snarls. It drives the young male back. The alphas show that they are in charge. The rest of the pack crowds around the leaders. They crouch down. They lower their tails and wag. Then they whine. Finally, it is their turn to eat.

Soon their stomachs swell with food. Wolves eat mostly meat. They eat until they can hold no more. Some wolves can eat up to 20 pounds (9 kg) of food at one time. They might not eat again for up to 12 days. It is important to get as much as they can when food is available. The pack is tired from the hunt. It is time to go home to the pups.

The pack slowly trots back. They enter the den as the sun rises. This cozy cave is where the pups were born. Wolves can have from one to 11 pups in each **litter**. At first, the pups are helpless. They weigh only 1 pound (0.5 kg) each. They cannot see or hear for the

◀ **Gray wolves snarl to defend their food.**

first few weeks. The pups grow quickly on their mother's rich milk. Soon they leave the den. They start to explore.

The pups sleep in a heap. Their tails move as they dream. Four of the pups have gray coats. The largest has coal-black fur. Gray wolves are the largest members of the dog family. They are the size and shape of German shepherds when full grown. Then they will weigh between 40 to 175 pounds (18 to 79 kg).

The pups' eyes snap open when the hunting pack members return. The pups rush up to the pack. The pups whine. They lick the hunters' noses. They beg for food. The adult wolves carry extra food in their stomachs. They bring up this food to their mouths to feed the pups. The pups gobble chunks of moose.

▲ **Gray wolves' fur can be gray, brown, white, or black.**

▲ **Pups spend a lot of their time playing with each other.**

The wolf that watched the pups also gets a meal. Soon the tired pack falls into a deep sleep. They have earned their rest. They will sleep all day. It will be 12 hours before they wake up.

Now the pups play. They chase their brothers and sisters. They pounce on each other. They tumble together. They wrestle. They nip at ears and tails. One pup finds an old bone. She tosses it in the air. Another pup grabs the bone. Then all the pups play keep away and try to grab the bone. The winner trots off with the prize bone. These games will help decide what each pup's rank will be in the pack. The strongest pup wins most games. One day, he will lead the pack as the alpha.

Chapter 3

GROWING UP

During the summer, the pups turn two months old. Now they are big enough to travel. The pack leaves the den. They find an open spot where they can live. It has more space for the growing pups. Here the pups explore. They are too young to join in a hunt. Instead they pounce on mice. This helps them learn hunting skills.

The new home is near the land where the pack hunts. It is also near water. Most wolves live in the wilderness. They live in northern areas of North America. Some also call Asia home. Some packs live in national parks. A pack's territory can be as small as 40 square miles (52 square hectares). Or it can be as large as 1,000 square miles (2,590 sq ha).

The pack needs to protect its new home. First, they patrol their land. Then they mark its borders. They do this by spraying their urine around the territory. They rub their scent on trees and rocks. This warns other packs to stay away. The wolves also howl.

◄ **Three pups explore their new space.**

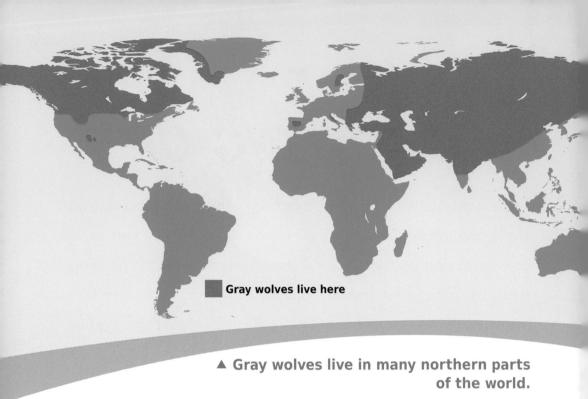

Gray wolves live here

▲ Gray wolves live in many northern parts of the world.

The summer days grow shorter. Soon it is autumn. The pack travels through the forest. The moose are on the move, too. The wolves need to stay close to their prey. They get ready to hunt. This time the pups join them. They are now six months old. It's time for them to start hunting.

All wolves are **predators**. They hunt, kill, and eat other animals. The pack works as one. Teamwork helps the wolves take down prey. The pack follows the signs from the alpha pair. The pair spots a lame moose. The pack focuses on its prey.

Other packs can hear a gray wolf's howl ▶ from 6 miles (10 km) away.

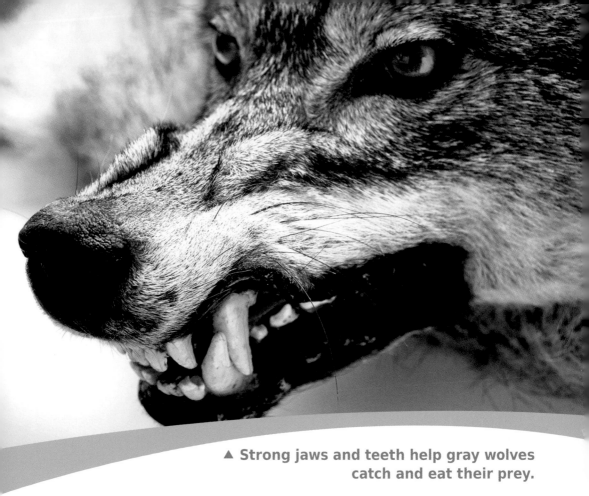

▲ **Strong jaws and teeth help gray wolves catch and eat their prey.**

All wolves are built to hunt. Their feet help them run fast. Their claws help them grip the ground. Wolves have very strong jaws. They grab the rear, side, or shoulders of their prey. They might also grip the nose or tail. Their teeth can tear flesh and hides. They can crush bones in a few bites.

First the alpha male chases the moose. The other wolves lie in wait. Then the alpha female takes over. The alpha male rests. One by one the other wolves wear out the moose. Finally the moose collapses. Then the pack eats its well-earned meal.

Soon the wolves have company at their meal. A flock of ravens join in the feast. The birds swoop down. They grab chunks of meat. But the wolves don't mind sharing. Sometimes the ravens lead them to prey. The big black birds also help protect wolves. They call out an alarm when danger is near. This helps warn the pack.

The wolf pups like to play with the ravens. They chase the birds. The two animals tease each other. The pups are now half-grown. They start to find their places in the pack. The biggest pup with the coal-black fur is bold. In time he could become the leader of the pack.

▲ **Ravens circle above prey, letting gray wolves know where prey can be found.**

Chapter 4

CHANGES

Winter arrives. Snow starts to fall, and the pack grows thick, winter coats. Wooly fur keeps them warm in the cold. Their coats can shed water. This stops snow from melting on their fur. The days are shorter now. At night the pack curls up to sleep. They cover their noses with their tails. That way their noses stay warm.

Hunting in winter is not as easy as summer hunting. The wolves live off the fat that they have stored from previous kills. This morning the wolves are howling. They are hungry. The pack needs to hunt.

The alpha male leads the pack. He follows a trail in the snow. Moose made the trail. The other wolves follow the leader. This helps them save energy. They walk in single file.

The wolves veer off the trail. They smell and hear a moose before they see it. Wolves have a strong sense of smell. They also have great hearing. They can hear 20 times better than humans.

◄ With their thick coats, gray wolves are built to handle winter weather.

▲ Gray wolves' feet fan out and act as snowshoes when running through the snow.

The pack needs to stay out of sight. They also need to stay upwind of their prey. That way the moose will not smell them. The pack swiftly runs through deep snow.

The alpha male sneaks up to the moose. The pups wag their tails. They are excited. They dash after the prey. They ruin the surprise attack. Now the moose turns. She is older. She fights hard. She kicks the alpha male. He is injured. The pack draws back. They return home hungry.

The alpha male's injuries are too serious for him to recover. He dies. Now is it the next strongest male's turn to be the alpha. He must lead his pack. He has many duties. Spring is just around the corner. His mate is pregnant. To prepare for spring and new cubs, the pack makes a new den. They use their claws to dig a **burrow** in the side of a hill.

In spring, the wolves welcome the new litter. Three gray pups grow quickly on their mother's milk. Wolf pups drink milk for about six weeks.

Now the five pups from last spring's litter are adults. The biggest pup prepares to leave the pack. He will seek out his own territory. He will travel hundreds of miles. In time, he will gather a new pack. Then he will become the alpha male. Together with the alpha female he will raise many litters of pups.

▲ **One pup of the litter will grow up to be the alpha male.**

GLOSSARY

alpha (AL-fuh): An alpha is the highest-ranking wolf in a pack. The alpha male and female are the first to eat after a hunt.

burrow (BUR-oh): A burrow is a hole in the ground made by an animal for shelter. The alpha female picked the location of the burrow where she would raise her pups.

den (DEN): A den is the home of a wild animal. Male and female adult gray wolves take turns watching the pups in the den.

litter (LIT-ur): A litter is a group of animals born to an animal at one time. The litter of wolf pups snuggled together for warmth.

mammals (MAM-uhlz): Mammals are warm-blooded animals that have hair or fur and produce milk for their live young. Gray wolves are mammals.

mate (MATE): A mate is one of a breeding pair of animals. Only the mate of the alpha male gives birth to pups.

predators (PRED-uh-terz): Predators are animals that eat other animals. Gray wolves are top predators.

prey (PRAY): Prey are animals that are eaten by other animals. Wolves work together to hunt large prey.

TO LEARN MORE

Books

Leaf, Christina. *Gray Wolves*. Minneapolis, MN: Bellwether Media, 2015.

Marsh, Laura. *Wolves*. Washington, DC: National Geographic, 2012.

Meinking, Mary. *Gray Wolves*. New York: Bearport, 2014.

Web Sites

Visit our Web site for links about gray wolves: childsworld.com/links

Note to Parents, Teachers, and Librarians: We routinely verify our Web links to make sure they are safe and active sites. So encourage your readers to check them out!

SELECTED BIBLIOGRAPHY

"Gray Wolf." *National Wildlife Federation*. National Wildlife Federation, 2015. Web. 4 June 2015.

"Wolf." *National Geographic*. National Geographic, 2015. Web. 7 June 2015.

"Wolf Reproduction and Maturation." *Western Wildlife Outreach*. Western Wildlife Outreach, 2015. Web. 6 June 2015.

INDEX

ABOUT THE AUTHOR

Nancy Furstinger is the author of more than 100 books. She has been a feature writer for a daily newspaper, a managing editor of trade and consumer magazines, and an editor at children's book publishing houses. She lives in Upstate New York with a menagerie of animals.